重庆第二师范学院重大委托课题"核心素养背景下儿童'融思促学'特色资源开发
T03)、重庆市社科规划项目"儿童英语阅读能力与思维技能双发展实验研究"(
重庆第二师范学院科研平台"儿童外语教育协同创新中心"(编号:201605)阶段研究成果

U0587491

小学英语
融思促学活动
设计与研究

周利君　向小婷　邹　娟　编著

重庆大学出版社

图书在版编目（CIP）数据

小学英语融思促学活动设计与研究／周利君，向小婷，邹娟编著. -- 重庆：重庆大学出版社，2020.11
ISBN 978-7-5689-2499-3

Ⅰ．①小…　Ⅱ．①周…　②向…　③邹…　Ⅲ．①英语课—教学研究—小学　Ⅳ．① G623.312

中国版本图书馆CIP数据核字（2020）第229765号

小学英语融思促学活动设计与研究

周利君　向小婷　邹　娟　编著

责任编辑：陈　亮　　版式设计：周永梅　陈　亮
责任校对：谢　芳　　责任印制：赵　晟

*

重庆大学出版社出版发行
出版人：饶帮华
社址：重庆市沙坪坝区大学城西路21号
邮编：401331
电话：（023）88617190　88617185（中小学）
传真：（023）88617186　88617166
网址：http://www.cqup.com.cn
邮箱：fxk@cqup.com.cn（营销中心）
全国新华书店经销
重庆俊蒲印务有限公司印刷

*

开本：787mm×1092mm　1/16　印张：7.5　字数：220千
2020年12月第1版　　2020年12月第1次印刷
ISBN 978-7-5689-2499-3　定价：45.00元

　　记得2011年，我在北京给小学教师做讲座的时候提到如何通过英语教学培养学生的思维能力，很多教师还不是很理解。当时主流的观点是：外语教学首先要培养学生的语言能力，要积累一定的语言技能、词汇、语法、句型等，然后才能谈别的方面。如果学生没有这些语言的基础，就无法培养思维能力。

　　实际上，学生从学习语言的第一天开始，就涉及思维能力的培养。我访问过好几所美国的小学，儿童在学前就已经开始进行思维能力的培养，比如区分"事实与观点（facts or opinions）"。几乎每所学校，都把要培养的几种思维能力，贴在教室墙上，这给我留下了深刻印象。

　　我想，初学英语的学生，虽然开始接触的语言很少，但是完全可以培养思维能力。举个例子：苹果有营养是"事实"，某种苹果最好吃是"观点"。只是我们的教师需要知道，应该培养哪些方面的思维能力，比如说：原因和结果、分类、推断、归纳等；更为重要的是：教师们还需要知道，如何培养这些思维能力，什么任务活动有助于培养这些思维能力，可以借助什么工具等。

　　最近几年，随着国家课程标准的修订，关于培养学生核心素养的要求已成为教师们讨论的热点话题，特别是品格培养和思维培养这两个方面。教师们感到，基础教育的目标应该是人的全面发展，必须培养学生的思维能力和品格。但是，究竟如何做，对思维的分类、内涵、范畴等，现在还缺乏明确的定义，更缺乏非常清晰的指导。到底培养学生哪些方面的思维能力，通过什么样的活动能培养这些思维能力，教师们缺乏现成的、方便实用的资料。我很高兴看到，重庆第二师范学院周利君老师带领的团队设计出这样一套适合小学高段学生和教师使用的小学英语融思促学活动资源。这真是及时雨！

　　这套活动资源的学生版可用于学生学习、亲子学习；教师版可用于教学的补充资源、校本课程，也可作为提高教师专业知识与能力的学习材料。所以在这里，一方面，我要对周老师及其团队表示衷心的祝贺；另一方面，也希望有更多的中小学英语教师能积极应用这套活动资源，将发展学生的思维能力、良好品格和行为习惯与培养英语运用能力结合起来。我也希望有更多的老师，能受到这套活动资源的启发，在自己的学校开展各种创造性的活动，共同铺建英语教育的新路。

龚亚夫

2020年7月4日

　　语言是思维的外壳，思维是语言的内在。核心素养背景下，学习者语言能力与思维能力同步发展成为广大一线教师开展英语教学改革与科学研究的重要课题之一。

　　布鲁姆等1956年提出的教育目标分类体系被国际教育界广泛采用。随着分类体系研究的发展，安德森等汇集认知心理学、课程研究、教育研究和语言测试等方面的研究成果，发布了更符合21世纪教育教学改革发展的教育目标分类体系修订版，主要包括认知过程和知识两个维度。其中，认知过程维度包括六大类别，每一类别下面又包含若干子类别的思维技能，形成由易到难、由简单到复杂的目标层次结构。相对于思维能力，思维技能理解难度系数低，以特定的思维理论框架作为英语教学的依托、涵盖不同层级思维技能的训练，在教学中具有更强的实操性。融入式思维教学将思维训练贯穿于学科日常教学中，与学科教学相辅相成。

　　2015年以来，重庆第二师范学院外国语言文学学院通过巴渝海外引智计划引进英国纽卡斯尔大学林梅博士和汉纳肯博士，联合开展"外语教育融思促学教研团队"（以下简称"团队"）建设，对合作基地小学优秀师资和院内英语师范专业优秀学子进行培养。在这个过程中，团队多次深入一线小学英语课堂教学观摩，发现小学英语教学多重语言知识技能，轻思维训练，其主要原因在于思维理论框架复杂且较抽象，缺乏教材配套思维训练资源。自

2018年开始，团队积极致力于外语教育融思促学资源开发。2018年年底，团队选送第一批完成的融思促学活动参加国家未来学校博览会，受到来自市内外参会一线教师的肯定与欢迎。团队大受鼓舞，结合在合作基地学校开展的融思促学实验研究开发了小学英语融思促学活动，供小学高段学生和教师使用。

本套活动资源教师版和学生版与以人教版为代表的现行小学英语教材（五年级）单元话题配套，从课标中各话题下语言知识和语言技能学习要求出发，提供语言知识学习和语言技能训练的活动。单元编写体例采用Top-down的语言学习理念，从语言技能到语言知识，整体特点鲜明，具体如下：

思维技能融入的显性化。显性化途径多元，一是在学生版和教师版的活动步骤中凸显思维技能的动词表达并不断重复，有助于师生理解和记忆。二是在教师版活动过程说明之后采用思维试纸，将活动步骤与对应的思维层级相匹配，有利于教师明确所设计活动的认知复杂度，并检查单元活动设计的思维层级的多样性。三是在活动步骤旁运用提示贴纸，凸显思维工具和策略的使用说明，促使教师有意识地引导学生借助思维工具和策略强化思维训练。

思维技能融入的具体化。针对一线教师在英语教学中融入思维训练太过抽象，不知道如何在课堂中实现这一问题，活动设计教师版从一线教师角度，模拟教案形式，对教学目标设定和教学活动步骤、教学建议等进行了具体说明，帮助教师快速进入融入式教学实践。部分活动步骤说明还提供了多种方案和实施建议，给予教师空间根据自身课堂情况进行筛选和调整。

思维技能融入的全面性。思维训练方面，依据修订版的布鲁姆教育目标分类框架的认知维度，覆盖低阶思维技能和高阶思维技能。结合各单元主题情境，教学活动设计兼顾基础思维技能活动和复杂思维过程任务，关注单个技能和复杂思维的同步训练。语言教学方面，每个单元采用从整体到局部的教学思路，从听、说、读、写等语言技能入手，落实到词汇、语法等语言知识的学习，满足不同的语言教学需求。

　　本套活动资源是重庆第二师范学院重大委托课题"核心素养背景下儿童'融思促学'特色资源开发"（批准号：2017XJZDWT03）、重庆市社科规划项目"儿童英语阅读能力与思维技能双发展实验研究"（批准号：2019YBJJ107）、重庆第二师范学院科研平台"儿童外语教育协同创新中心"（编号：201605）阶段研究成果，由课题负责人周利君组织设计、主持编写、审校定稿。其中5A部分由邹娟、周利君编写完成，5B部分由向小婷、周利君和陈慧贤编写完成。贺倩彧、孙亮参与统稿，部分活动由单芳、邹若环在合作基地小学进行了课堂实践后提出修订建议。本套活动资源编写过程中，得到了重庆第二师范学院外国语言文学学院领导和同事、巴渝海外引智专家、基地学校领导和同行的大力支持，在此表示衷心感谢。

　　由于课题组成员水平有限，难免有错漏之处，敬请各位专家和同行批评指正。

周利君

2020年7月

Contents

目 录

5A

5B

Unit 1 What's He Like?

Part One Listening and Speaking

I. Listening Comprehension

1. Listen and **tick** which teacher they are talking about.

   A. Ms. Wang.   B. Mr. Li.

2. Listen again and **fill in** the blanks with words to describe what the teacher is like.

      _____ is _____ and sometimes _____.

II. Preparation before Speaking

1. We have 3 new teachers. Choose proper word(s) from the Word Box and put down the letters to **match** the pictures.

> **Word Box**
>
> A. old   B. young   C. strict   D. funny   E. hard-working
>
> F. kind   G. clever   H. shy   I. polite   J. tall

_____   _____   _____

2. Read the introductions below about the 3 teachers and **find out** the similarities (相同点) and differences (不同点) between the words you choose and the words in the introductions.

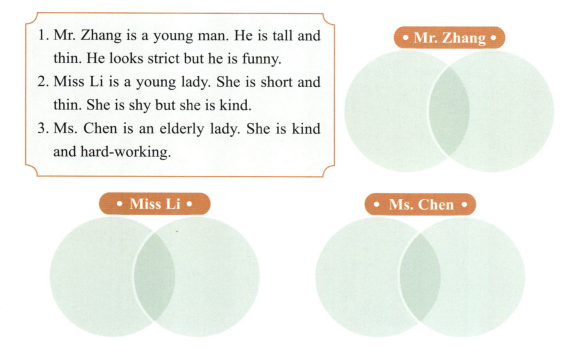

1. Mr. Zhang is a young man. He is tall and thin. He looks strict but he is funny.
2. Miss Li is a young lady. She is short and thin. She is shy but she is kind.
3. Ms. Chen is an elderly lady. She is kind and hard-working.

• Mr. Zhang •

• Miss Li •

• Ms. Chen •

III. Speaking and Sharing

1. Discuss and **make** a list of the features of your favorite teacher.

My favorite teacher is _____.
She / He is...

kind
...

2. **Make** a profile (简单描述) for an ideal English teacher.

Name:
Gender:
Age:
Height:
Subject:
Personality:

3. **Introduce** the teacher you create to the class.

An ideal English teacher should be / have

_____ .

Word Box

pretty / beautiful	slim
patient	loving
friendly	warm-hearted
helpful	sympathetic
competent	knowledgeable

Part Two   Reading and Writing

I. Preparation before Reading

Brainstorm: What a robot is like in a bubble map.

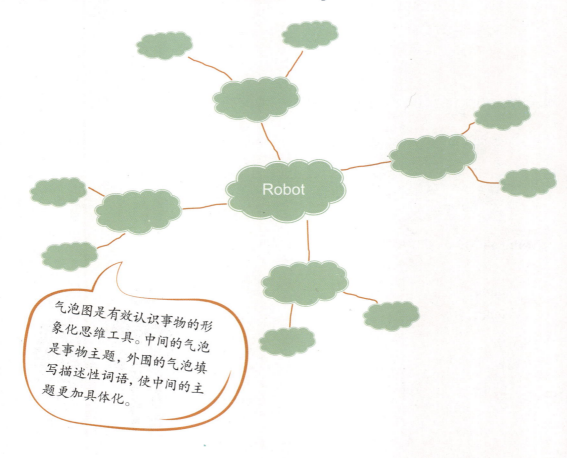

气泡图是有效认识事物的形象化思维工具。中间的气泡是事物主题，外围的气泡填写描述性词语，使中间的主题更加具体化。

II. Reading Comprehension

1. Read and **underline** the robot's name and his creator.
2. Read and **complete** the bubble map about Robin.

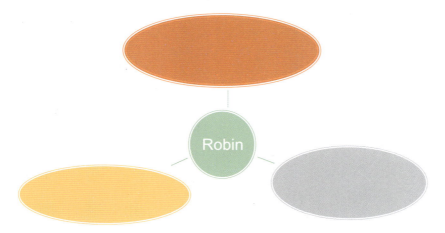

III. Preparation before Writing

Write to **describe** the features and functions of the robots in the pictures.

He can _____ .
He is _____ .

He can _____ .
He is _____ .

IV. Writing and Sharing

Design a robot for your mother by drawing and writing a short introduction.

This is a robot for my mother because she is _____.

He is a / an _____ robot.

He is / can _____

_____

_____

_____

_____

Part Three   Vocabulary

I. Word Searching

Circle the 5 words in this unit hidden in the word puzzle. The first one has been done for you.

b	a	u	m	i	n	t	o	n	d
w	h	e	l	p	f	u	l	z	i
c	h	y	e	t	a	h	a	l	f
s	e	o	s	y	f	u	n	n	y
t	z	u	e	a	t	r	a	k	e
r	n	n	l	d	i	n	g	o	r
i	c	g	t	i	v	e	h	u	e
c	j	w	o	k	e	p	t	l	n
t	r	a	s	h	y	a	r	d	t

II. Word Pairs

Classify the words in the box into pairs.

> **Word Box**
>
> old   short   thin   clever   shy
>
> lovely   tall   strong   young   out-going
>
> smart   cute

(1) _____ _____   (2) _____ _____   (3) _____ _____

(4) _____ _____   (5) _____ _____   (6) _____ _____

Part Four　Grammar

I. Self-checking

Read the pictures (读图) below and **make** sentences (造句).

What's _____ like?
_____ is _____ .

What's _____ like?
_____ is _____ .

II. Further Practicing

Select words or phrases to **match** the pictures.

— What's _____ like?

— _____ is _____.

— What's _____ like?

— _____ is _____.

— What's _____ like?

— _____ is _____.

a man	funny
30	shy
helpful	she
a woman	strong
hard-working	strict
he	

Unit 2 My Week

Part One Listening and Speaking

I. Listening Comprehension

1. **Predict** the lessons John has on Thursday and what Grandpa does on Thursday based on the picture in the textbook.

> John has _____ on Thursday.
> Grandpa has _____ on Thursday.

2. Listen and **fill in** the blanks.

> John has _____, _____ and _____ on Thursday.

> Grandpa has _____ on Thursday.

3. Listen again and **complete** the sentences.

> _____ is John's _____ teacher.
> . He is _____.

II. Preparation before Speaking

Read Wu Yifan's weekend schedule and **discuss** how he feels on the weekend and why.

Wu Yifan's Weekend Schedule

	Saturday	Sunday
9:00–11:00	Math	English
13:00–15:00	Handwriting	Art
18:00–20:00	Chinese Writing	Piano

— How does Wu Yifan feel on the weekend?

— I think he is _____ on the weekend because...

III. Speaking and Sharing

1. **Brainstorm** on the activities a good weekend schedule should have with your group.

   A good weekend schedule should have _____.

2. Report in groups the ideas to the whole class and **agree on** some key ideas.

   A good weekend schedule should have
   _____.

3. **Identify** and circle what should be changed in the schedule.
4. **Change** the parts you identified with your group and explain the reasons.

Before → Now

Language Kit

Wu Yifan has _____ on _____ before. Now we change it into _____, because he likes _____.

    He _____ on _____ before. Now we add _____, because _____.

Part Two   Reading and Writing

I. Learning before Reading

Read the pictures in the textbook and **tick** how Wu Yifan is feeling at the moment.

Wu Yifan is...

happy ☐	excited ☐	sad ☐	tired ☐
sleepy ☐	angry ☐	hungry ☐	

II. Reading Comprehension

1. Read and **find out** what Wu Yifan is feeling at the moment and why.

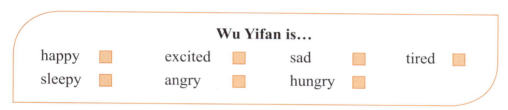

Wu Yifan is _____ because _____.

2. Read and **tick** what he often or sometimes does on weekend and **cross** what he doesn't.

(1) do sports ☐   (2) watch TV ☐

(3) read books ☐   (4) play games ☐

3. **Evaluate** his schedule and decide what is good and what is not good.

It is good to have
_____ because
_____ .

It is not good to have
_____ because
_____ .

III. Preparation before Writing

Compare the following schedule of an American primary school with yours, and put down the similarities and differences in the double bubble map.

Schedule					
	Monday	**Tuesday**	**Wednesday**	**Thursday**	**Friday**
8:50–9:00	Arrival	Arrival	Arrival	Arrival	Arrival
9:00–9:30	Morning Meeting	Morning Meeting	Morning Meeting	Morning Meeting	Morning Meeting
9:30–10:10	Math	Math	Math	Math	Spanish
10:10–10:55	Snack / Recess	Snack / Recess	Snack / Recess	Snack / Recess	Snack / Recess
10:55–11:25	Reading and Writing	Reading and Writing	Music	Reading and Writing	Reading and Writing
11:25–12:00	Reading and Writing	Reading and Writing	Spelling	Reading and Writing	Class Meeting
12:00–1:00	Lunch / Recess	Lunch / Recess	Lunch / Recess	Lunch / Recess	Lunch / Recess
1:00–1:30	Handwriting	Spelling	Handwriting	Spelling	Science
1:30–2:00	Class Meeting	Science	Science	Science	Science
2:00–2:45	Violin	Art	Dance	P.E.	Reading Partners
2:45–3:00	Pack up / Closing	Pack up / Closing	Pack up / Closing	Pack up / Closing	Pack up / Closing

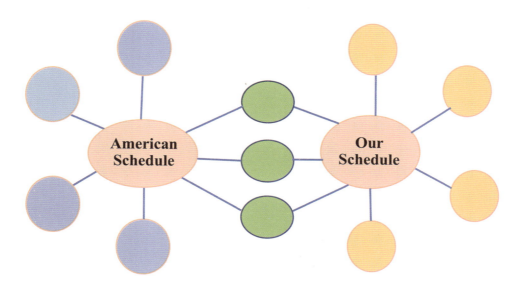

IV. Writing and Sharing

Write down at least 3 similarities and 3 differences between the two schedules.

Language Kit

We both have… (on…)

They have… on…, but we have…

They have… but we don't have…

Part Three　　Vocabulary

I. Self-checking

Choose the correct word in brackets to complete the following sentences.

(1) The two kids are (washing / watching) TV.

(2) Anna is (looking / washing) clothes.

(3) I often (read / look) books on weekend.

(4) Do you like (playing / reading) football?

(5) My classmates sometimes (do / make) homework in the classroom.

II. My Daily Activities

1. **Record** the time needed for your daily activities.

Activity	Day	Time Needed
washing clothes	**Saturday**	**20 minutes**

Language Kit

wash clothes, watch TV, do homework,
read books, have class and play football

2. **Arrange** the activities from the most time needed to the least and decide whether it is good or not.

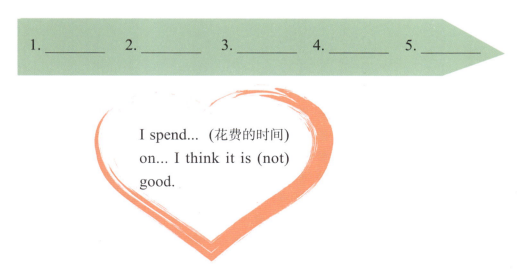

1. _____   2. _____   3. _____   4. _____   5. _____

I spend... (花费的时间) on... I think it is (not) good.

Part Four   Grammar

I. Self-checking

Complete the sentences based on your school schedule.

What do you have in a week?

I have _____, _____, and _____ on Wednesday.

I have English on _____, _____, and _____.

I have _____ every day.

What do you do in a week?

I _____ on _____.

I _____ every day.

II. Information Gap Activity

Complete Wu Yifan's school schedule **using** the sentence structures:

What does he have on…?

He has…

Monday	Tuesday	Wednesday	Thursday	Friday

A版

Monday	Tuesday	Wednesday	Thursday	Friday
Science	Chinese	Math	Art	English

B版

Monday	Tuesday	Wednesday	Thursday	Friday
Math	English	Chinese	P.E.	Computer

Unit 3   What Would You Like?

Part One   Listening and Speaking

I. Listening Comprehension

Listen and **complete** the form.

Who	What would he / she like to eat? Why?	What would he / she like to drink? Why?

II. Preparation before Speaking

Read the menu and **make** an order for the 2 children.

I just played basketball. Now I'm thirsty and hungry! I like meat.

I'm hungry. I want to have some fast food and desserts.

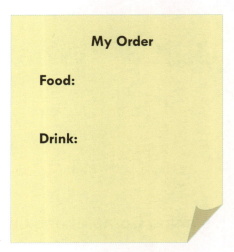

Food	Drink
sandwich	tea
hamburger	water
salad	Cola
ice cream	milk
noodles	juice
beef	coffee
fruits	
vegetables	
chicken	

My Order

Food:

Drink:

III. Speaking and Sharing

1. Discuss and **evaluate** the food in your orders with group members and **decide** the final order in your group.

> **Language Kit**
> What would you like?
> I'd like some… for…
> It is good for you because it is delicious / healthy / children's favorite.

2. **Share** the final order of your group to the class.

> This is our order for the 2 children. We'd like some… for… because she / he is… and it is…

Part Two　Reading and Writing

I. Preparation before Reading

Rank the following food from what you like least to most.

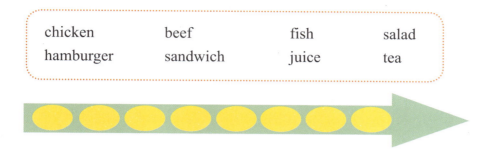

chicken	beef	fish	salad
hamburger	sandwich	juice	tea

II. Reading Comprehension

1. **Identify** the addressers (写信人) and addressees (收信人) of the two letters in the textbook.

Letter 1
Addresser: _____
Addressee: _____

Letter 2
Addresser: _____
Addressee: _____

2. Read and **put down** what Wu Yifan likes and dislikes in the left bubble, what Grandpa likes and dislikes in the right bubble, and what they both like in the middle part.

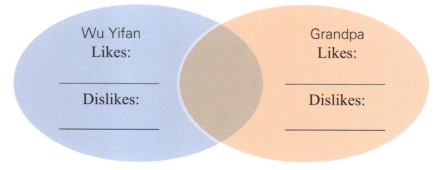

Wu Yifan
Likes:
_____
Dislikes:
_____

Grandpa
Likes:
_____
Dislikes:
_____

3. **Think about** why they say no to Robin's dish.

They say no because _____.

III. Preparation before Writing

Your friend Simon invites your parents and you for dinner and he wants to know what you like and dislike. **Put down** what you like and what you don't like in the table.

Who	Likes	Dislikes

IV. Writing and Sharing

Write a letter to Simon and tell him what your family would like to eat and drink and what you would not like and give reasons.

Language Kit

I don't like to eat / drink… but… is OK.

I like to eat / drink… but not…

Dear _____,

_____

_____

_____

Thank you!

_____

_____

Part Three   Vocabulary

I. Self-checking

Fill in the blanks with appropriate letters to complete the words.

(1) Hamb__ __ger is d__l__cious.

(2) S__l__d is fre__ __ and h__ __lthy.

(3) Sandwi__ __ is deli__ __ous.

(4) __ __ __ cream is sw__ __t.

(5) T__a is h__t.

II. My Refrigerator

Let's help Mom to **categorize** the following food and put them in the right part of her refrigerator.

| beef | egg | noodles | chicken | onion |
| milk | carrots | cheese | yogurt | cucumber |

III. My Cooking

Decide what ingredients (配料) are needed for the dishes and put down appropriate words in the blanks.

chicken hamburger   _____

beef noodles   _____

vegetable salad   _____

egg sandwich   _____

Part Four　Grammar

I. Self-checking

Complete the sentences with appropriate words.

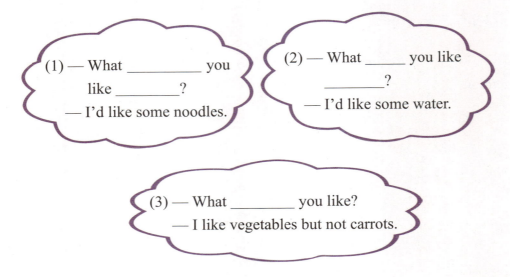

(1) — What _____ you
like _____?
— I'd like some noodles.

(2) — What _____ you like
_____?
— I'd like some water.

(3) — What _____ you like?
— I like vegetables but not carrots.

II. Rule-finding

Summarize the sentence patterns for the functions.

Ordering food and drink:
_____

Expressing likes or dislikes:
_____

III. Further Practicing

Find out what the people in the pictures would like to eat / drink according to the given information.

She'd like _____.

She'd like _____.

He'd like _____.

Unit 4   What Can You Do?

Part One   Listening and Speaking

I. Listening Comprehension

Listen and **fill in** the blanks.

(1) Zhang Peng can _____.   (2) John can _____.

II. Preparation before Speaking

1. **Find out** what your group members can do for the English party.

Name	Can

2. **Design** a program list for a one-hour English party for the National Day celebration of our school based on the table you just filled.

English Party

Grade: _____   Class: _____   Date: _____   Time: _____

Program	Performers	Time

By Group _____

III. Speaking and Sharing

1. **Share** your English party program list to the class.
2. **Evaluate** and vote for your favorite one and explain the reasons.

> **Language Kit**
> I think my favorite one is _____
> because _____.

Part Two   Reading and Writing

I. Preparation before Reading

1. Chain game: I can do it!
Students work in groups to **act out** what different animals can do with body language and ask if the one sitting next can do it.

> — I am a penguin and I can turn my head. Can you do it?
> — I can do it.

2. Supposing you have a robot, draw what it is like and **fill in** the bubble map what it can do.

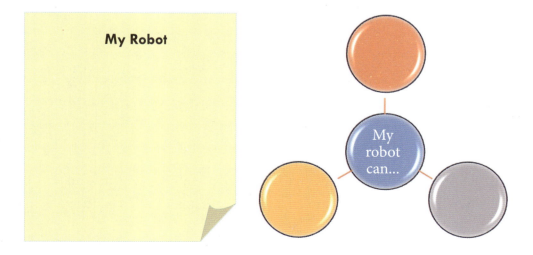

My Robot

My robot can...

II. Reading Comprehension

1. Read and **list** what Robin the robot can do and can't do.

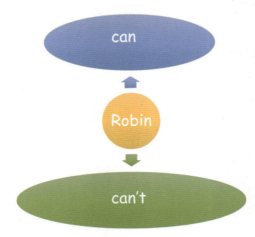

2. **Compare** Robin and the robot you described, and complete the double bubble map to present the similarities and differences.

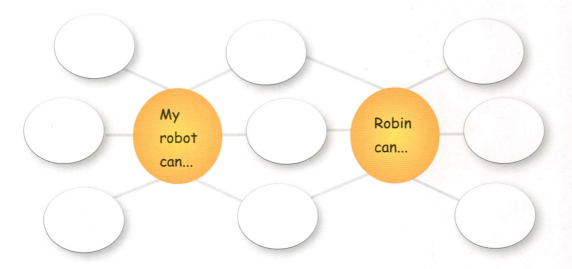

III. Preparation before Writing

Good friends should have something in common. Talk to your deskmate and see if you can **find** at least 3 things that you and your deskmate both can do and neither can do in the chart. If you can, you can be good friends.

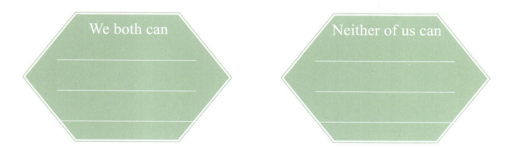

IV. Writing and Sharing

1. **Write down** the things both your deskmate and you can do.

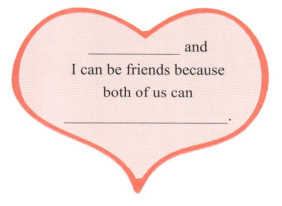

2. **Write** an email to one of your classmates to tell him / her 3 things that you can't do and ask him / her for help.

Dear _____,

_____

_____

_____

_____

_____

Yours,

_____

Part Three   Vocabulary

I. Let's Bingo!

dance

sing English songs

do kung fu

draw cartoons

play the pipa

swim

speak English

play basketball

cook

play ping-pong

play football

play the piano

II. Complete the Vocabulary Mind Map

Part Four   Grammar

I. Self-checking

Make sentences to share if you and your family members can do the things listed in the box.

What can you / he / she do?

dance	sing English songs	do kung fu
draw cartoons	play the pipa	swim
speak English	play basketball	cook
play ping-pong	play football	play the piano

(1) I (can / can't) _____. (2) My mother (can / can't) _____.

(3) My father (can / can't) _____. (4) My grandpa (can / can't) _____.

(5) My grandma (can / can't) _____.

II. Rule-finding

Circle what shares in the above sentences (圈出上述句子中相似的地方).
Summarize the sentence patterns.

Sentence Patterns:

III. Further Practicing

Judge whether the following sentences are correct in grammar. If it is correct, tick (√)
it. If not, cross (×) it and write the correct sentence on the line.

(1) He can plays basketball. (   ) _____

(2) She can play the piano. (   ) _____

(3) Tom can does kung fu. (   ) _____

(4) Jenny can cooking. (   ) _____

Unit 5　There Is a Big Bed

Part One　Listening and Speaking

I. Preparation before Listening

1. **Guess** a riddle.

> You can clean me up, but you can't move me.
>
> You can dress me up, and you can live in me.
>
> What am I?

2. **Brainstorm**: What there is / are in a living room.

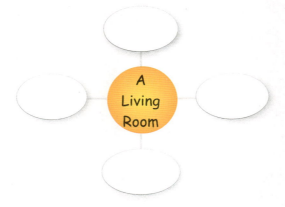

II. Listening Comprehension

1. Listen and **tick** what room it is.

    ▢ bedroom　　　　▢ study　　　　▢ living room　　　▢ kitchen

2. Listen and **tick** what there are in the room.

    ▢ some pictures　　▢ some plants　　▢ some toys　　　▢ some flowers

III. Preparation before Speaking

Fill in the blanks based on the picture in the textbook.

	Objects in the Living Room		
pictures	There are some _____ ; they are _____ the TV.		
plants	There are some _____ ; they are _____ the window.		
books	There are some _____ ; they are _____ the bookshelf.		
fish	There are some _____ ; they are _____ the fish bowl.		
dogs	There are two _____ . The yellow dog is _____ the table, and the black dog is _____ the table.		
...	...		

IV. Speaking and Sharing

1. Wu Yifan's family is moving into a new house. Can you **design** a bedroom for him?

2. **Describe** what there is / are in your bedroom, **evaluate** your designs and decide on the best design in your group.

> **Language Kit**
> There is a TV in the front of the living room.
> There are some / many…
> in / on / under / above / in front of / beside / between

3. **Share** the best design of your group to the class.

> Hello, everyone! We are glad to introduce our group's best design for Wu Yifan's bedroom. There is / are…

Part Two   Reading and Writing

I. Preparation for Reading

What's different?

Contrast and describe the differences between Picture A and Picture B.

A

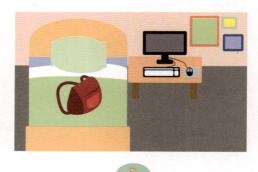

B

Language Kit

There are 2 books on the bed in Picture A but there is a schoolbag on the bed in Picture B.

There is… while there isn't any…

II. Reading Comprehension

1. Skim to **match** the objects to their positions in Mr. Jones' room.

computer	on the floor
pencils and crayons	behind the computer
pictures and photos	in front of the mouse
mouse	everywhere

2. **Think about** why Mr. Jones ask for help and how would Robin help him. Put down your ideas in the two charts.

III. Preparation before Writing

Mr. Jones left the messy room. Now Robin will help Mr. Jones to **relocate** the objects in the room to make it clean and tidy. Can you help him?

Objects	Positions Before	Positions Now
pencils and crayons		
pictures and photos		
mouse		

IV. Writing and Sharing

Write an email to Mr. Jones to tell him the room is clean and tidy now, and describe the room to him.

Dear Mr. Jones,

    I am Robin the robot. Your room is _____ now.

_____

_____

_____

                                            _____

                                  _____

Part Three   Vocabulary

I. Word Searching

Circle the 7 words of the objects in the room. The first one has been done for you.

b	a	y	m	i	n	t	o	n	d
w	w	i	n	d	o	w	l	z	i
c	h	u	p	t	a	h	a	l	f
p	e	c	h	y	b	o	o	k	s
l	z	l	o	a	t	r	a	k	e
a	n	o	t	b	o	t	t	l	e
n	c	c	o	i	v	e	h	u	e
t	j	k	s	k	e	p	t	l	n
s	r	a	b	i	k	e	r	d	t

II. Blank-filling

Complete the sentences according to the pictures on Page 51 of the textbook, using the words in the box.

The pictures _____ _____ the wall.
The bookshelf _____ _____ the TV.
The black dog _____ _____ the table.
The plants _____ _____ the chairs.
The books _____ _____ the bookshelf.

beside	above
in front of	between
on	behind
under	

Part Four   Grammar

I. Self-checking

Complete the sentences with proper words.

(1) There _____ a book on my table.
    There _____ some books on my table.
(2) There is a _____ in my schoolbag.
    There are some _____ in my schoolbag.

II. Rule-finding

1. **Circle** what shares in the above sentences.
2. **Summarize** the sentence patterns.

III. Further Practicing

Describe the objects and their positions in your home.

(1) There is _____.

(2) There are _____.

(3) _____

(4) _____

(5) _____

My Home

Unit 6　In a Nature Park

Part One　Listening and Speaking

I. Preparation before Listening

1. **Tick** the nature park from the following three pictures.

2. **List** the differences in the three kinds of parks.

II. Listening Comprehension

1. Listen and **decide** whether the statements are True or False.

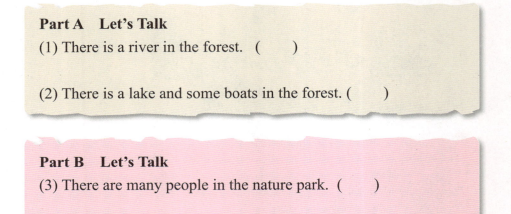

Part A   Let's Talk

(1) There is a river in the forest.   (   )

(2) There is a lake and some boats in the forest. (   )

Part B   Let's Talk

(3) There are many people in the nature park. (   )

(4) There are some animals in the nature park. (   )

(5) There are many tall buildings in the nature park. (   )

2. **Find out** what there is / are in a nature park.

There is / are   in a nature park.

III. Preparation before Speaking

Each student prepares a picture of their favorite nature park, and **mark** what there is /
are in the nature park.

IV. Speaking and Sharing

1. Students work in pairs to **complete** a picture of a nature park by asking questions.

Language Kit

Is there a… in the nature park?

Are there… in the nature park?

Where is the…?

It is beside / near / in front of the…

2. **Decide** if the following things are a part of a nature park. Share your ideas in your group and tell why or why not.

wild animals	rivers	mountains	tents
merry-go-round	garbage	playground	lakes
roller-coaster	trees	grassland	

Language Kit

I think… is / are a part of a nature park because…

I don't think… is / are a part of a nature park because…

Part Two   Reading and Writing

I. Preparation for Reading

Predict where Robin is and what is he looking at.

Who?	Robin
Where?	
What?	

II. Reading Comprehension

1. **List** what Robin sees in the nature park.

2. **Find out** the locations of what there is / are in the nature park.

(1) There is _____ the village.
(2) There is _____ Mr. Jones' house.
(3) There are _____ the lake.
(4) There is a high _____ the park.
(5) There is _____ the mountain.

III. Preparation before Writing

List what you would like to see in a nature park and **design** a nature park.
A group of American visitors are going sightseeing in China. Recommend them a Chinese nature park by drawing a picture of it.

IV. Writing and Sharing

1. Write to **describe** what there is / are in the nature park you recommend and the locations.

> The nature park is _____. There is / are
> _____ in the nature park. _____
> the nature park, there is / are _____
> _____.

2. **Find** your "friend": Ask your group members if they and you have the same things in your nature parks. If you have more than 3 things in common, you are "friends".

> — What are there in your nature park?
> — There is / are _____ in my nature park.

Part Three   Vocabulary

I. Self-checking

Write down what there is / are in a nature park in the blanks.

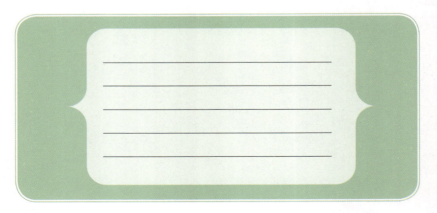

II. Word Searching

Circle the 8 words in this unit hidden in the word puzzle and write them in the blanks. The first one has been done for you.

b	a	m	o	u	n	t	a	i	n
w	h	e	l	p	f	u	l	z	i
c	b	u	e	t	a	h	a	l	f
f	r	n	s	y	l	a	k	e	y
o	i	g	e	a	t	r	a	k	e
r	d	b	u	i	l	d	i	n	g
e	g	e	t	i	v	e	h	u	e
s	e	w	h	o	u	s	e	l	n
t	r	a	h	i	l	l	r	d	t

(1) __hill__

(2) _____

(3) _____

(4) _____

(5) _____

(6) _____

(7) _____

(8) _____

Part Four　Grammar

I. Self-checking

Fill in the blanks to complete the conversation in pairs and draw a picture of a nature park based on the conversation.

— Is there a high _____ in the nature park?

— Yes, there is.

— _____ wild animals in it?

— Yes, there are. There are _____.

— _____?

— Yes, there is, and there is a bridge on it.

— Are there any people in the nature park?

— _____. It is very quiet.

II. Rule-finding

Circle what shares in the above sentences.
Summarize the sentence patterns and the usage of them.

III. Further Practicing

1. Here are some sentences about your hometown Chongqing. **Judge** whether the
   following sentences are correct in grammar. If it is correct, tick it. If not, cross it
   and correct the mistake.

(1) There are a river in Chongqing. (　　　)

(2) There is many bridges in Chongqing. (　　　)

(3) — Are there any boats on the river? (　　　)

　　— Yes, there is. (　　　)

(4) Is there a tall mountain in Chongqing? (　　　)

(5) Is there trees in the mountain? (　　　)

(6) On front of the mountain, there is a village. (　　　)

(7) There are many places of interest in Chongqing. (　　　)

(8) — Are there many tall buildings in Chongqing? (　　　)

　　— No, there are. (　　　)

2. A 10-year-old American boy would like to visit some cities in China. **Write** a short paragraph to recommend Chongqing to him.

　　　Chongqing is my hometown. There…

Unit 1   My Day

Part One   Listening and Speaking

I. Listening Comprehension

1. Listen and **fill in** the blanks.

so

Mom _____ last night, ⟶ Sara is _____ today.

2. Listen again, **tick** what Sarah does on the weekend and then fill in the blanks.

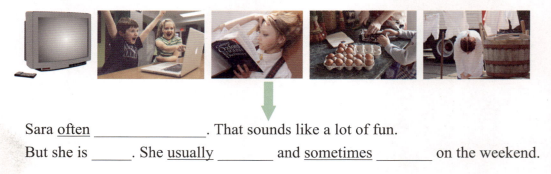

Sara <u>often</u> _____. That sounds like a lot of fun.

But she is _____. She <u>usually</u> _____ and <u>sometimes</u> _____ on the weekend.

II. Preparation before Speaking

Recall and **write** down what you normally do on Saturday morning.

Give 1–5 stars to what you do to show the importance (重要性).

	Saturday	Importance
6:00–7:00	e.g. sleep	(☆☆☆☆☆)
7:00–8:00		

	Saturday	Importance
8:00–9:00		
9:00–10:00		
10:00–11:00		
11:00–12:00		
12:00–13:00		
13:00–14:00		
14:00–15:00		
16:00–17:00		

III. Speaking and Sharing

You're going to have a picnic in the park on Saturday with three of your friends for three hours. You have different time schedules (时间表), but you need to **decide** when you can have the picnic together.

1. **Analyze** (分析) your own time schedule and think about when you will be free (有空) and when you can change your plan (改变计划) to go to the picnic. Write down "√" (can go for a picnic), "×" (cannot go for a picnic), or "?" (not sure 不确定) beside each time period in your time schedule.

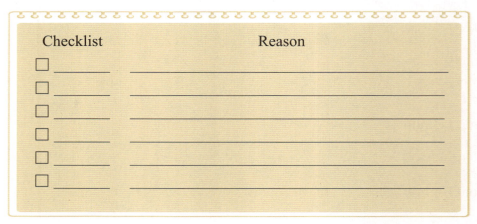

Checklist	Reason
☐ _____	_____
☐ _____	_____
☐ _____	_____
☐ _____	_____
☐ _____	_____
☐ _____	_____

2. **Recommend** the proper time for your picnic and **explain** your reasons in group discussion. Fill in the form when sharing your ideas.

Names				
First Choice				
Second Choice				

You can **use** the sentence patterns below to discuss.

> **Language Kit**
>
> My first choice is…, because I am free from... to…
>
> I (do sth.)… from… to…
>
> My second choice is… because I (do sth.)… from... to... I can change (改变) it.

3. **Compare** (比较) your choices and circle the same choice(s). Then **decide** the time for picnic and **explain** why you make this decision.

Let's go for a picnic

from   to

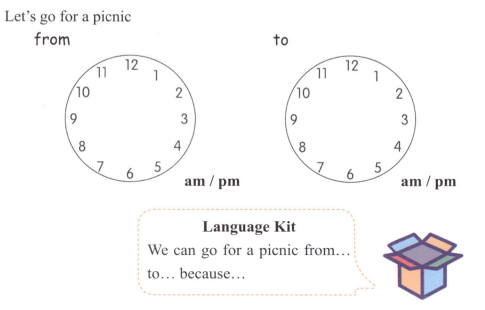

am / pm   am / pm

Language Kit

We can go for a picnic from…
to… because…

Part Two   Reading and Writing

I. Preparation before Reading

Imagine a person is living on the island based on the picture and **brainstorm** what he does in the morning and in the afternoon.

Use what you know to guess and fill in the forms below.

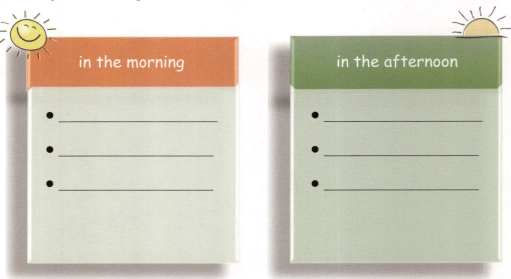

II. Reading Comprehension

1. After you read Robin's play, **underline** what Robinson does in a day. **Match** them to your guessing, and tick the same ones in the above forms. Share in groups about how you find the answers.

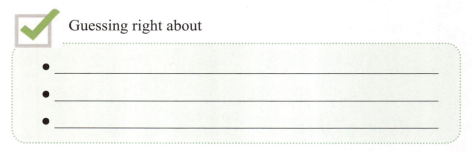

Guessing right about

- _____
- _____
- _____

2. **Match** and **fill in** the blanks with the activities of Robinson and **color** the column to **show** the frequencies. The more you color, the more frequent it is.

		0 (不涂)	100% (涂满)
always	_____		
sometimes	_____		
often	_____		

III. Preparation before Writing

1. **Recall** and **list** the activities you do every day (weekday and weekend), and **compare** them with Robinson's and write them down in the chart.

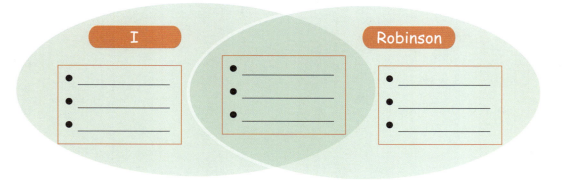

2. **Mark** your feelings when you do the activities by drawing the emojis (表情) beside them and **select** the ones you want to share with Robinson.

   For example:

| happy | sad | angry | excited | bored |

3. Are you satisfied with your day? Do you want to change some activities? **Write down** your evaluation here and **explain** why.

   I do not want to _____. I want to _____,

   because _____.

IV. Writing and Sharing

1. What do you want to share with Robinson? **Write** about your day and your ideas.

Dear _____,

  My name is _____. I am a student.

We share a lot in common. We _____.

We _____ ... I am _____.

But, I_____ I _____...

I am _____. I like / dislike _____.

I want to _____, because _____ ...

Yours,

_____

Language Kit

写信过程中，如果你想要知道对方的想法，可以使用"What about you?" "Do you like…/ dislike…?"等问句。

2. Challenge yourself! Is there a person you like living in other countries? Let's **share** your life and ideas with him / her.

- Who is him / her? What does he / she do?
- Where is he / she living now?
- What does he often / sometimes / always do in his / her daily life?

 What do you feel about his / her life?

Part Three   Vocabulary

I. Checking Your Memory

Match the pictures to the phrases below and each one can be used once only. Write down the matching number of the picture in "( )".

do morning exercises (   )   eat breakfast (   )   have… class (   )
play sports (   )   eat dinner (   )   clean my room (   )
go for a walk (   )   go shopping (   )   take a dancing class (   )

(1)

(2)

(3)

(4)

(5)

(6)

(7)

(8)

(9)

II. Further Comprehending

Classify these phrases into different groups and **explain** the reasons. You need to use up all the phrases and classify them into 2 groups at least. Write down the picture numbers into different group circles. You can add more circles if you need more groups.

Group name: _____   Group name: _____

Part Four   Grammar

I. Self-checking

1. The words below represent frequency. **Link** them to the matching percentage (%).

sometimes   usually   always   often

100%   80%   60%   40%

2. **Choose** one from "sometimes / often / usually / always" to **fill in** the blanks. And share yours with your partner.

I _____ have dinner at home.

I _____ go shopping.

I _____ have English class.

I _____ clean my room.

（注意：这几个频度词可以重复使用，符合实际情况即可。）

II. Further Practicing

Choose the suitable person / pet to do suitable activities with you.
And **make** sentences with the sentence pattern and phrases below.

> What do you / they do on the weekend?
>
> _____ (who) _____ (frequency) _____ (activity)
> with _____ (who) on Saturdays / Sundays.
>
> **do morning exercises**   **eat breakfast**   **have… class**
>
> **play sports**   **eat dinner**   **clean my room**
>
> **go for a walk**   **go shopping**   **take a dancing class**
>
> 注意: 造句时只替换 "sometimes / often / usually / always"几个频
> 度副词，不算新的句子。要根据不同的身份，选择恰当的事情进行
> 匹配，造句意思要合理，要符合常识。

Let's see how many sentences you can make.

Dad   Brother   Sister   Mom   Cat   Dog

(1) _____

(2) _____

(3) _____

(4) _____

(5) _____

(6) _____

(7) _____

Unit 2　My Favorite Season

Part One　Listening and Speaking

I. Listening Comprehension

1. Listen and **fill in** the blank with seasons.

    Miss White likes _____ best.

2. **Match** Amy and Miss White to the pictures of their favorite seasons and **recall** the reasons why they like the seasons best. Pictures can give you clues (线索).

Amy

Miss White

II. Preparation before Speaking

1. **Think** which season you like best in Chongqing. Why? Write down your answers in the form below. You can add more aspects by yourself.

My favorite season in Chongqing is _____.	
Weather	It is…
Color	There are…
Activities	I can… with…
Food & Drink	I can eat / drink…
Clothes	I can wear…
Add More	

2. Look at the pictures below. Can you **design** one for your favorite season in Chongqing?

　　Tip: 下列图片是如何把文字和季节相关的元素结合起来的？先思考，再设计。

Draw your logo here!

III. Speaking and Sharing

1. Each student **ticks** the best season in Chongqing in their own mind.

◇ spring

◇ summer

◇ autumn / fall

◇ winter

2. Discuss in groups and **explain** your decisions in the form below. You can add more aspects by yourself.

Tip：每个方面要明确写出这个季节不同于其他季节的特点。

We think the best season in Chongqing is _____.

	It is the best, because it is special in... (☺在……方面是特别的)
Weather	It is…
Color	There are…
Activities	We can… with…
Food & Drink	We can eat / drink…
Clothes	We can wear…

3. Choose one of the group members' pictures to **revise** and make it better. **Draw** it here.

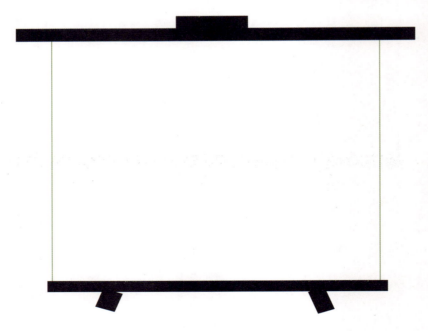

Part Two   Reading and Writing

I. Preparation before Reading

1. When are "four seasons" in Chongqing? Based on your knowledge, **recall** the name of each season in the middle circle for Chongqing.
   For example:

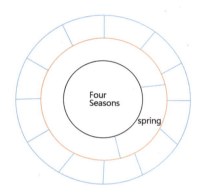 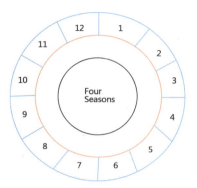

2. **Learn** the "Tip". Then **write down** the names of each season in the middle circle for Chongqing again.

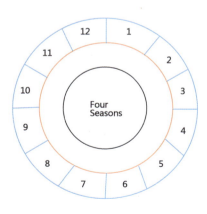

Tip:

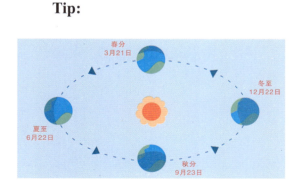

3. **Apply** what you have learnt, and **find out** which season it is. Write your answer in brackets and tick the matching weather.

   15/08 in Chongqing (   )   It is warm / cool / hot / cold.

   01/10 in Beijing (   )   It is warm / cool / hot / cold.

   24/01 in Canada (   )   It is warm / cool / hot / cold.

4. **Test** your partner.

_____ in _____ is _____.

It is _____.

5. **Challenge** yourself!

02/02 in Thailand   (   )   12/25 in Australia   (   )

It is warm / cool / hot / cold.   It is warm / cool / hot / cold.

II. Reading Comprehension

1. Read and **pick out** words from the box to fill in the blanks.

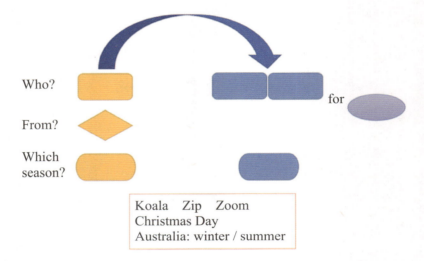

2. **Read** again and **answer** the questions.

(1) Which season does Koala like?

  A. Spring.   B. Summer.   C. Autumn.   D. Winter.

(2) What does not Koala do on Christmas Day?

  A. Go to the beach.   B. Swim in the sea.   C. Make a snowman.

  Why? _____

III. Preparation before Writing

Recall and **compare** the colors you see on the Spring Festival in Jilin province and Hainan province in China and fill in the form below.

Hainan

Jilin

Language Kit

White for snow. Because in winter, it often snows in Jilin.

Yellow for sand. Because we often go to the beach in Hainan and play with sand.

…

Jilin

Hainan

ALIKE

Red for lanterns (灯笼)

_____

_____

DIFFERENT

White for snow
_____
_____
_____
_____

Yellow for sand
_____
_____
_____
_____

IV. Writing and Sharing

Choose colors to best **represent** the Spring Festival for your hometown. **Write** about them and **explain** the reasons of your choices.

I think _____ (colors) can represent the Spring Festival for my hometown _____ (province or city name). _____ is for _____; _____ is for _____; _____ is for _____

_____

_____

I choose them because _____

_____

_____

_____

(climate / activities / environment).

Language Kit

Climate: It is… / It… / It has… in winter.

Activities: We make a snowman / have dinner with family… on the Spring Festival.

Environment: There are… flowers / trees…

Part Three   Vocabulary

I. Checking Your Memory

Select phrases from the box and **match** these pictures.

A. _____

B. _____

C. _____

D. _____

E. _____

F. _____

G. _____

make a snowman; go swimming;
go on a picnic; play in the snow;
eat ice cream; pick apples
plant flowers

II. Matching and Comprehending

Analyze clues and write down the seasons or activities in the first row.

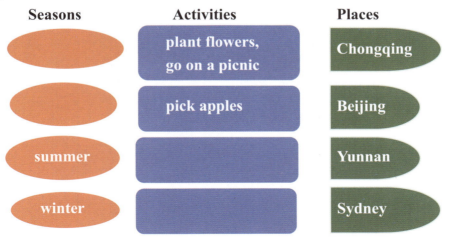

Seasons	Activities	Places
	plant flowers, go on a picnic	Chongqing
	pick apples	Beijing
summer		Yunnan
winter		Sydney

III. Using Vocabulary

1. Answer the question "Which season do you like best?" **Recall** and fill in the blank.

I like _____ best.

2. **Select** the phases in Exercise 1 to **explain** your idea, and write down the letters (字母) in the blank.

Because I can _____.

3. **Write down** other reasons.

Because _____

_____.

Part Four   Grammar

I. Self-checking

Analyze the picture clues below and **make** sentences with "what", "when", "where", "which", and "why".

— _____?
— _____ is in the box.

— _____?
— I like _____ best.
— _____?
— Because _____.

— _____?

— I wake up _____.

— _____ on the weekend?

— I often _____.

II. Rule-finding

Circle what shares in the sentences and fill in the blanks. Cross the words of the first column.

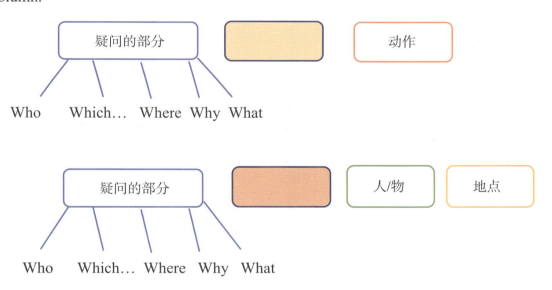

III. Further Practicing

Students can work in pairs and **use** question and answer to **draw** a picture including: who, when, where, what.

Unit 3   My School Calendar

Part One   Listening and Speaking

I. Preparation before Listening

There is a school trip in Beijing. Can you **guess** when and where students will go? Write down your ideas in the columns below. You can draw if you do not know the words.

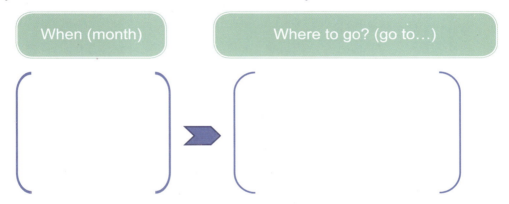

When (month)   Where to go? (go to…)

II. Listening Comprehension

Listen and **fill in** the columns.

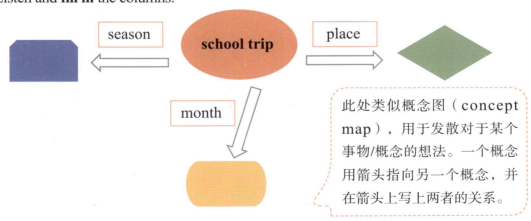

season   school trip   place   month

此处类似概念图（concept map），用于发散对于某个事物/概念的想法。一个概念用箭头指向另一个概念，并在箭头上写上两者的关系。

III. Preparation before Speaking

Identify and circle what are included for planning a day trip.

IV. Speaking and Sharing

1. **Brainstorm** and **analyze** what your mom likes and what she dislikes.

Likes	Dislikes

2. **Design** a trip plan for your mom to celebrate Mother's Day.

海报中要包含 "Daily Trip Planner"的主要内容。

Part Two   Reading and Writing

I. Preparation before Reading

Recall festivals and holidays and write them down on your school calendar.

School Calendar

January	February	March	April	May	June
July	**August**	**September**	**October**	**November**	**December**

II. Reading Comprehension

They are primary school students in America. We're going to invite them to our school. They can stay here for one month.

But in which month should they come?
What can they do?
Let's find it out together!

Look at their school calendar. **Tick** what are the same as ours. **Circle** what are different. Write down our different festivals and holidays into each month.

III. Preparation before Writing

Select the best three months for those American primary school students to come. **Explain** the reasons.

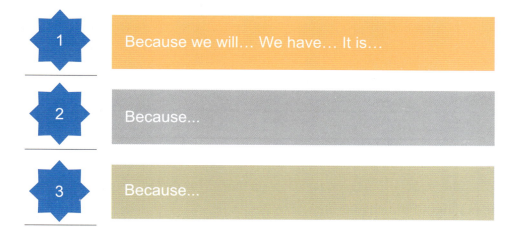

IV. Writing and Sharing

Choose the best month and **write** the invitation.

You are invited!

When:
Why:

Where:
What:

Part Three　Vocabulary

I. Word-checking

Put months into the right column and **correct** the wrong spellings.

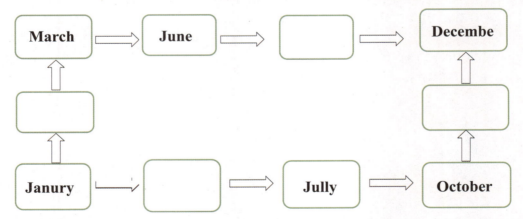

II. Naming and Matching

Write down the festival name under each picture. **Match** festivals to months. Write down the number of months beside festivals.

(1) _____   (2) _____   (3) _____   (4) _____

(5) _____   (6) _____   (7) _____   (8) _____

III. Further Associating

Choose one month and list the festivals below. Let's compete who can **think of** the most festivals and **recall** relevant (相关的) activities.

Month:

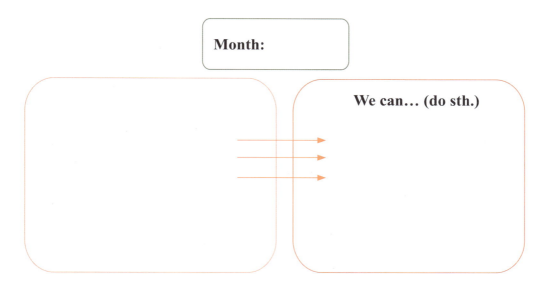

We can… (do sth.)

Part Four　Grammar

I. Self-checking

Recall your birthday and fill in the blanks.

When is your birthday?

It is _____ _____;

It is ____on____ _____;

It is _____ _____ o'clock.

Choose from "in", "at", "on".

II. Rule-finding

Collect three more birthdays from your family or your classmates.

Who: _____

in / on / at	month	month	month
	date	date	date
	o' clock	o' clock	o' clock

III. Further Practicing

You are going to hold a birthday party for these three persons together. **Choose** the time and answer these questions by filling in the blanks.

When is the birthday party?

_____ (month) _____ (date) _____ (o'clock).

Because _____.

What will you do?

We will _____.

Unit 4   When Is the Art Show?

Part One   Listening and Speaking

I. Preparation before Listening

Look and **identify** the date.

May 2020					
Sun	Tue	Wed	Thu	Fri	Sat
				1	2
3	5	6	7	8	9
10	12	13	14	15	16
17	19	20	21	22	23
24	26	27	28	29	30
31					

When is May Day?

May Day is on _____ _____.

II. Listening Comprehension

1. **Recall** and write down the special days in May.

_____.

2. Listen and **judge** the statements are True or False.

(   ) (1) The art show is on May 3rd.

(   ) (2) May Day is on May 1st.

(   ) (3) The reading festival is on May 7th.

3. Do you know other special days? **Recall**, fill in the blanks and share.

I know _____.

Time: It is on _____.

Place: We often _____.

Activity: We can _____.

III. Preparation before Speaking

1. We have some special events in June. You are invited to choose one and plan an event for our class.

Events in June			
Children's Day	Environment Day	the Dragon Boat Festival	Father's Day

2. **Plan** your festival and **fill in** the blanks. Try to attract the guests.

(1) What event do you choose to plan?

We choose _____.

(2) When is it?

It's on _____,

because _____

_____.

(3) Where will it be held?

It's _____.

(4) What activities do you have?

We have _____

_____.

> singing show, kung fu show, dance competition, you do and I guess…

(5) What can the guests do?

They can _____

_____

_____.

> dance, sing, draw, write, do kung fu, eat, drink, watch TV, listen to music, run, jump, cook, play football / basketball…

3. Let's **make** a poster for your event. **Draw** and **write**. You should cover information from the 5 questions in Exercise 2.

IV. Speaking and Sharing

1. Let's **share** and invite your classmates to join in your event. The more stars you get, the more popular is your party! Let's see: whose event is the most attractive.

Speaking pattern:

Invitation

Event:
Date:
Place:
Activities:

You can:

Dear Friends,
 Welcome to our _____. It's on _____. It's _____.
We have _____ for you. You can _____.
 Please join us!

Invitation

2. Count the stars and **choose** the most attractive group.

Children's Day	Environment Day	the Dragon Boat Festival	Father's Day
Group _____	Group _____	Group _____	Group _____

Part Two   Reading and Writing

I. Preparation before Reading

Sarah has some new kittens. Here are some pictures of the kittens. **Order** these pictures and draw a line.

| April 21st | April 15th | April 26th | May 3rd |

II. Reading Comprehension

1. Sarah writes a diary about her kittens. Read the diary and **find** the kittens' change. Please **finish** the flow map (流程图) below.

Time	Age	Feature	Ability
On _____	they are _____	They are _____. Their _____ are _____.	They can / can't _____.

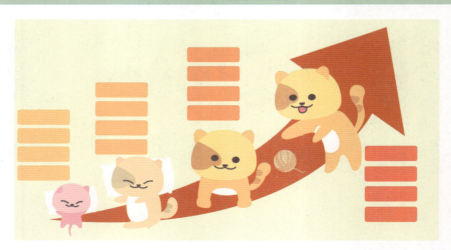

2. **Investigate** the answer according to the picture in Exercise 1.

(1) Sarah has _____ new kitten(s).

    A. one   B. two   C. three

(2) Kittens are _____ because they are very young.

    A. pink   B. blue   C. white

(3) On April 21th, they can _____.

    A. run   B. make noise   C. walk

(4) Their eyes are open on _____.

    A. April 15th   B. May 3rd   C. April 26th

(5) The kittens can walk on _____.

    A. April 15th   B. May 26th   C. May 3rd

III. Writing and Sharing

1. **Choose** 2 pictures showing your mom or dad's changes and **sequence** (排序) the pictures according to the age, and then fill in these blanks.

    a photo of him / her before you born   a photo for now

_____. (age)   _____. (age)

_____ is _____.
_____ is / are _____. (feature)

_____ is _____.
_____ is / are _____. (feature)

2. What are his / her changes? Please observe and **summarize**.

Changes	Before	Now
appearance: (He is…) (His… is / are…)		
abilities: (He can.. / He can't…)		

3. **Write** a diary for your mom / dad now.

   You should consider:

   When is it today?

   How old is he / she?

   What is he / she like?

   What can he / she do?

   What he / she can't do?

   What does he / she like?

   What do you want to say to him / her?

4. **Share** your diary with your group members voluntarily.

Part Three   Vocabulary

I. Comprehending and Blank-filling

1. **Analyze** the form and **finish** the table.

one	first	1st
two		2nd
three	third	
four		
	fifth	
		6th

2. **Recall** and **write** the abbreviations (缩写) of the dates.

March second	January first	August third	June fifth

Mar. 2nd   _____   _____   _____

February twelfth	May twenty-first	April thirtieth	July fourth

_____   _____   _____   _____

II. Make Your Schedule

1. **Relate** your daily life this month and **fill in** the month column below.

2. Let's **make** a schedule for your life. **Check** on your schedule. Tick if the event is completed, and cross if it is not completed.

Month:

Sunday Monday Tuesday Wednesday Thursday Friday Saturday

Part Four　Grammar

I. Self-checking

1. When are these special days? Please **find** and **circle** the date on the calendar.

Tree Planting Day　　Father's Day　　Mother's Day　　National Day　　birthday

2. Look at the calendar and **finish** the sentences.

(1) — When is Tree Planting Day?

　　— It's _____ March 12th.

(2) — _____ _____ National Day?

　　— _____ _____ October _____.

(3) — _____ _____ Mother's _____?

　　— _____ on _____ _____.

(4) — _____ _____ _____ _____?

　　— _____ _____ _____.

(5) — _____ _____ your birthday?

　　— _____ _____ _____ _____.

II. Rule-finding

1. **Circle** what shares in the sentences on both sides below.

Find the Rules

When is Tree Planting Day?	It's on March 12th.
When is Mother's Day?	It's on May 12th.
When is Father's Day?	It's on June 16th.
When is National Day?	It's on October 1st.
When is your birthday?	It's on October 26th.

2. **Summarize** the sentence patterns.

The sentence patterns:

III. Further Practicing

Use the words in the box to make the sentences correct.

(1) — _____ is your birthday?

— It's on September 25th.

(2) — When is Teachers' Day?

— It's _____ September 10th.

(3) — Where is she?

— She is _____ home.

(4) — _____ can you do on the party?

— I can drink some Coke.

(5) — When is your mother's birthday?

— _____ on December 27th.

A. on   B. When
C. What   D. at
E. It's

Unit 5   Whose Dog Is It?

Part One   Listening and Speaking

I. Brainstorm

Based on your experience and knowledge, fill in the bubble map to **brainstorm** common dogs' behaviors in the daily life.

II. Listening Comprehension

Tick the right answer for each question.

(1) What is the name of the dog?

    A. Fido.   B. Fado.

(2) Whose dog is it?

    A. Sam's.   B. Chen Jie's.

(3) Where is the dog now?

    A. In the kitchen.   B. In the park.

(4) What is the dog doing?

    A. Drinking water.   B. Eating.

III. Preparation before Speaking

1. Imagine you have a lovely dog. What is it like? Take out a piece of paper and **draw** a picture of your dog. Here are some examples for you.

You should consider:

What is it like?

Where is it?

What is it doing?

2. Please **describe** your dog. Look and finish the sentences.

(1) What is it like?

It is _____.

> Appearance (外表): big, small, tall, long, short, strong…
> Color: black, white, brown, yellow, gray…
> Other: cute, lovely, naughty (调皮的)…

(2) Where is it?

It is _____.

> in the park, at home, on the street (在街上)…

(3) What is it doing?

It is _____.

> running, walking, jumping, eating, drinking, sleeping, climbing…

IV. Speaking and Sharing

1. Share your description to your group members. After listening and sharing, each group **chooses** one picture and give to the host. (The host needs to stick all the pictures on the blackboard.)

2. Now go to the Lost and Found (失物招领处). Each group chooses one reporter to **retell** the description.

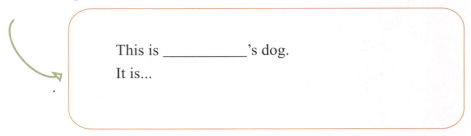

> This is _____'s dog.
> It is...

3. After each group has described it, the host points at the picture one by one, and interviews other students: Whose dog is it? Other students listen and **find** the dog's owner. (If the answer is right, he can get a medal (勋章) for helping.)

Part Two   Reading and Writing

I. Preparation before Reading

1. Have you ever been to a zoo? **Recall** what you saw in the zoo. Please share with your deskmates.

2. Today Robin and Sarah want to guide you to experience being an animal keeper. Let's take a look.

(1) In the morning, Sarah needs to feed the animals. What animals are in the zoo? Look at the picture in the textbook and **circle** their names in the box.

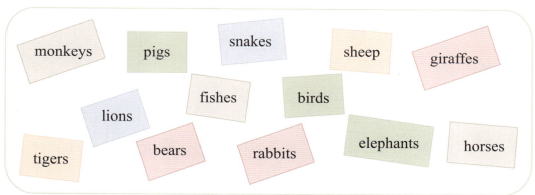

monkeys　pigs　snakes　sheep　giraffes

fishes　birds

lions

tigers　bears　rabbits　elephants　horses

(2) Sarah doesn't know what they eat in the zoo. Can you help her? Please **classify** the animals according to the food, and share with us.

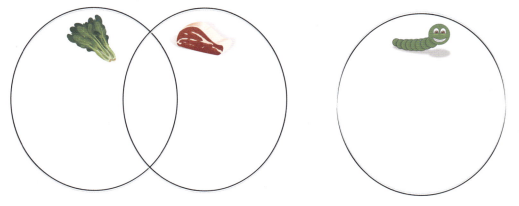

II. Reading Comprehension

1. After feeding, Robin needs to make sure the animals are OK. Let's find out what they are doing. **Match** and finish this table.

What animals do you see?	What are they doing?

walking

swimming

flying

climbing

dancing

running

eating

2. **Guess** why Robin doesn't want to swim like a fish. Write down the key words.

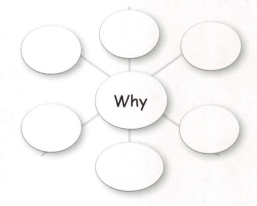

III. Writing and Sharing

1. What is your favorite animal in the zoo? Please write its name in the blanks, **explain** the reason, and share with us.

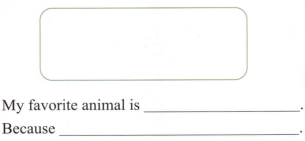

My favorite animal is _____.

Because _____.

2. What does your favorite animal look like? Please **describe** the features and **fill in** the table and share with us.

Feature	Description
eyes	
nose	
tail	
body	
color	
...	

3. At the end of the experience, **complete** your animal observation report.

> Your findings should include:
>
> (1) What animals do you see and what are they doing?
>
> (2) Which animal is your favorite, and what does it eat and look like?

My Observation (我的观察记录)

Name: Time:

(1) Animals:

_____

_____

_____

(2) Findings:

_____

_____

_____

_____

_____

Part Three　Vocabulary

I. Recalling

Look at the dogs. What are they doing? **Recall** and write the words under the pictures.

II. Matching and Writing

1. In the park, there are so many dogs. Whose dogs are they? **Match** the dogs to the owners and finish the table.

Owner	Dog
Hank	
Pam	
Helen	
Ben	
Tim and Tom	

2. **Read** the above table, and **apply** the words below to complete all the sentences.

> my　your　his　her　our　your　their

> mine　yours　his　hers　ours　yours　theirs

Dog A is <u>Helen's</u> dog. It is <u>her</u> dog. It is <u>hers</u>.

Dog B is _____ dog. It is _____ dog. It is _____.

Dog F is _____ dog. It is _____ dog. It is _____.

Dog G is _____ dog. It is _____ dog. It is _____.

Dogs C, D and E are _____ dogs. They are _____ dogs.
They are _____.

Part Four　Grammar

I. Finding Differences

1. Look at the two pictures. Can you **find** 3 differences? Please circle them out and share with us.

Find 3 Differences

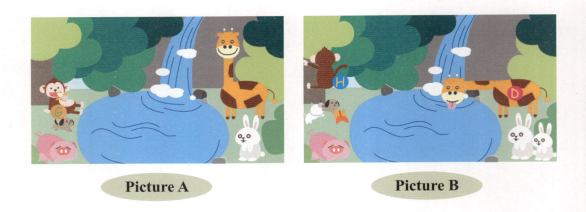

Picture A   Picture B

2. **Fill in** the blanks according to the above pictures.

(1) — What is Giraffe D doing?

— Giraffe D _____ _____ .

(2) — What _____ the dogs _____ ?

— The dogs _____ _____ .

(3) — _____ _____ Monkey H _____ ?

— _____ _____ _____ .

(4) — _____ is _____ _____ ?

— _____ _____ eating.

II. Rule-finding

1. **Circle** what shares in the sentences on both sides below.

Find the Rules

What is the pig doing?	The pig is sleeping.
What is the giraffe doing?	The giraffe is drinking.
What are the dogs doing?	The dogs are running.
What are the rabbits doing?	The rabbits are jumping.

2. **Summarize** the sentence patterns.

The sentence patterns:

III. Further Practicing

Look at the picture and choose 3 animals to test your partners. You can **use** the above sentence patterns.

1) — _____?
— _____.

2) — _____?
— _____.

3) — _____?
— _____.

Unit 6　Work Quietly!

Part One　Listening and Speaking

I. Listening Comprehension

1. Look at the picture and **select** where Tom is.
   A. In the classroom.
   B. On the playground.
   C. In the library.

2. Tom sees a boy. Let's listen to the conversation between them and **find out** what the boy's name is.

   His name is _____.

3. Listen and **tick**. What Tom should pay attention?

 A.　　　　　B. 　　　　　C.

II. Preparation before Speaking

1. At the beginning of the school, the students came to the classroom. Look at this classroom. What can you see? Please **identify** and share with your friends.

I can see _____.

2. Do you like this classroom? Why? Please **judge** and **write** your reasons.

> I _____ (like / don't like) this classroom.
> Reason 1:
> Reason 2:
> …

3. Should we make rules for the classroom? Please **judge**, **write** your reasons and share with your group members.

> I think we _____ (should / shouldn't) make rules for the classroom.
> Because…

4. If you are the monitor of this class, please think about what rules you can make. **Use** the sentence patterns and share with us.

> Rule 1:
> Rule 2:
> Rule 3:
> Rule 4:
> …

Sentence patterns:
No + doing (e.g. No eating!)
Keep + *adj*. (e.g. Keep clean.)
Do + *adv*. (e.g. Talk quietly.)

III. Speaking and Sharing

1. The principal (校长) gives you a task. You need to **introduce** the school to the first-grade students to help them understand the rules better.

| library | dining hall | computer room | playground |

2. One group chooses one place. Think and **write** the key words of that place.
   You should consider:

   Where is it?

   What can they do?

   What cannot they do?

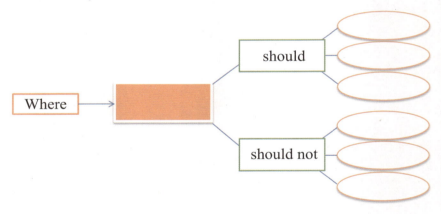

You can add more.

3. Each group presents the thinking map in class, and other group members will be the principals to **evaluate** the proposals (提案) and **explain** the reasons. After the presentation, each group needs to **amend** (修改) the proposals.

> I think it is good / bad. Because…
>
> (If it's bad) They should change (the bad one) to…

4. Let's regroup and **introduce** your place to the new group members. Other students need to **draw** at least 2 thinking maps while listening.

> Hi, I am your guide. I will introduce this place to you. Here is _____.
> Here are some rules: One…; Two…
> You can… here.

5. What do these places have in common? **Compare** your maps and then write them down.

Part Two   Reading and Writing

I. Preparation before Reading

Today there is a world robot exhibition. Robots come from many countries. Can you send each robot to the corresponding country's booth? **Match** robots to the countries.

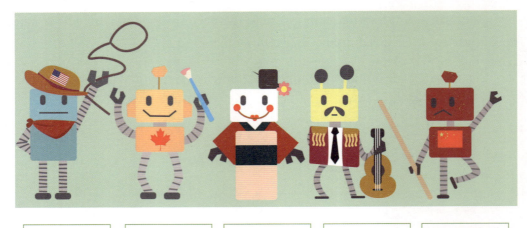

| Japan | Spain | U.S.A. | China | Canada |

II. Reading Comprehension

1. On the exhibition, what are the robots doing? **Read** and **choose**.

(1) The Canadian robot is _____.

(2) Asako is _____.

(3) The Spanish robot is _____.

(4) The Chinese robot is _____.

(5) Robin is _____.

drawing pictures

singing

making sushi

eating sushi

listening to music

playing music

doing kung fu

doing exercise

2. What can the English robot do, and why? **Brainstorm** and **explain** the reasons.

He can _____, because _____.

III. Writing and Sharing

1. In the next year, we still have the world robot exhibition. Can you design a robot which shows the Chinese features? What are Chinese features besides kung fu? **Brainstorm** your ideas.

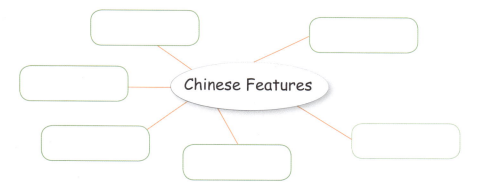

Chinese Features

2. How will your robot show these features?

   Think about the following questions and list your ideas.

(1) What action he / she is doing? **Read** the pictures and **write** your choice in the box.

play   listen   eat   do kung fu   drink   sing   dance   draw pictures

He / She is _____.

(2) **Choose** what dress he / she wears.

    Hanfu (汉服)

    Qipao (旗袍)

    Chinese tunic suit (中山装)

    …

(3) **Choose** what he / she holds in hand.

    fan (扇子)

    sword (剑)

    flute (笛子)

    …

3. Let's **design** a new robot to show Chinese features. **Draw** it below.

Robot Introduction

Name: Color: Size:

In the picture:

_____

My robot can also:

_____

_____

4. Introduce your robot with your group members. Let's **choose** the robot that best fits the Chinese features. And **summarize** the reasons below.

> We think _____'s robot is the best.
> The reasons are:
> (1)_____
>
> _____
> (2)_____
>
> _____
> (3)_____
>
> _____

Part Three   Vocabulary

I. Understanding and Blank-filling

Did you see these signs in real life? What do they mean? Please **match** and write.

Talk quietly.	Keep to the right.	Keep your desk clean.
No touching!	No feeding!	No eating!
No climbing!	No smoking!	

①

②

③

④

_____   _____   _____   _____

⑤

⑥

⑦

⑧

_____   _____   _____   _____

II. Rule-matching

For different places, we have different rules. Please **categorize** (分类) the rules in different places. Write the number in the blanks and share with us.

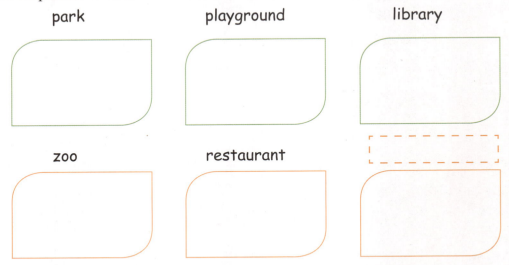

park   playground   library

zoo   restaurant

III. Rule-making

In our classroom, do we have rules? Let's **make** rules for our class. Please **draw** the sign and write the meaning.

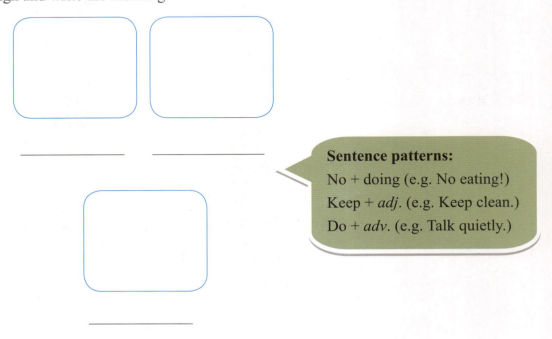

Sentence patterns:

No + doing (e.g. No eating!)

Keep + *adj*. (e.g. Keep clean.)

Do + *adv*. (e.g. Talk quietly.)

Part Four   Grammar

I. Comprehending and Blank-filling

What are the children doing? Discuss and **fill in** the blanks.

This is my photo.

This is me. I _____ _____.

These are _____ and _____. They _____ fighting.

This is Lily. She _____.

This is Mike. He _____ _____.

This is Tom. _____ _____ _____.

II. Rule-finding

1. **Circle** what shares in the sentences on both sides.

Find the Rules

What are you doing?	I am running.
What is she doing?	She is sleeping.
What is he doing?	He is drawing.
What is it doing?	It is drinking water.
What are you doing?	We are playing.
What are they doing?	They are having English class.

2. **Summarize** the sentence patterns.

The sentence patterns:

III. Further Practicing

1. **Classify** the words and put them in the right boxes.

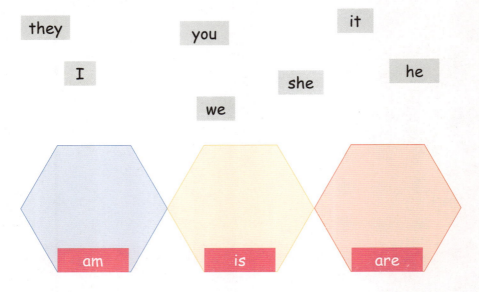

2. Now you are an English teacher. You need to **find** and **correct** the mistakes in the following exercises. Can you find them?

(   ) (1) — What are you doing?

—I _____ running.

A. am   B. is   C. are

(   ) (2) — What is she doing?

— She _____ sleeping.

A. are   B. does   C. is

(   ) (3) — What _____ you doing?

— We are playing.

A. am   B. is   C. are

(   ) (4) The children _____ football.

A. is playing   B. are playing   C. am playing

(   ) (5) Listen! She _____ in the classroom.

A. is singing   B. is sing   C. to sing

(   ) (6) Jack and Kitty _____ in the pool. Let's join them.

A. is swimming   B. am swimming   C. are swimming